CAPRICORN

HOROSCOPE

& ASTROLOGY

2021

Published by Mystic Cat Press

Suite SM-2380-6403

14601 North Bybee Lake Court

Portland, Oregon 97203

Phone: +1 (805) 308-6503

SiaSands@yahoo.com

Copyright © 2020 by Mystic Cat Press

Contents

Acknowledgment:

To my family, thank you for being there and accepting my wildness.

Dedicated to those with an open heart, an open mind, and a willingness to plumb the mysteries of life.

You make this world a better place.

CAPRICORN 2021
HOROSCOPE & ASTROLOGY

Capricorn

Capricorn Dates: December 22nd to January 19th
Symbol: Goat
Element: Earth
Planet: Saturn
House: Tenth
Colors: Brown, Grey

2021 inspires and delights with three gorgeous Supermoons in the first half of the year. New opportunities arrive, which will breathe fresh air into your surroundings. Exciting joint projects are likely, this sees your social circle expanding, and offers many opportunities to embrace happiness and connection in your life. A wake-up call arrives to improve your confidence, it leads you towards a time where you focus on developing the romance and passion in your life. It highlights the potential possible when you remain steadfast and committed to achieving your personal goals. This puts the spotlight on a significant situation that holds substantial promise in your life. Unique and inspiring options are revealed in 2021.

On February 12th we ring in the Chinese New Year of the Ox, this is an important event, the magic, arrives to allow you the ability to harness the power of manifestation. Your inspiration is fueled by a sense of security and abundance, which comes to bolster your spirits. You enter a productive time, which sends you trailblazing towards realizing a vital goal. Your creativity is peaking with fresh sparks to be developed.

Mercury Retrograde gets up to tricks in 2021, you are especially sensitive to cosmic vibrations, and you begin to feel some cosmic fallout. You start the process of clearing up old emotions that have been cluttering up your life. It's through this process that you will be able to find the clarity that you have been searching for. Consider this as a help for you to find the direction you are seeking. Time is needed to find a clear path forward. Doing this inner work enables you to go through a time of evaluation, self-assessment, and re-balancing.

Solar eclipses can only occur during a New Moon phase. This is when the Moon moves between Earth and the Sun, and these three celestial bodies form a straight line: Earth–Moon–Sun.

A Lunar eclipse occurs when the Earth stands between the Moon and the Sun. This obscures the light of the Sun from the Moon. The Moon herself has no light source of her own, as she simply reflects the light of the Sun. A lunar eclipse occurs during a Full Moon and usually marks endings, transitions, or other life cycle culmination points.

Any eclipse is a significant event in astrological circles, eclipses have fascinated scientists for centuries. Eclipses are dramatic tools that instigate change in your life. An eclipse is wild, free, expansive, and explosive, the wild cards of astrology, you never quite know what you get until it happens. An eclipse can uproot, surprise, inspire, motivate, and really become an active catalyst for change. Eclipses remove the shutters, they make you aware of areas that need to be changed and often spotlight an entirely new direction to explore. Eclipses inspire change and work rapidly to see forward motion occurring.

WORKING WITH THE MOON

2021 delights with three gorgeous Supermoon's. A supermoon is when the Moon is at its closest approach to Earth, which occurs during a full or new moon. The effect on the ocean's tides is most significant when there is a full or new moon. This tidal force is concentrated during the super Moon, it can cause the ocean tides to rise by an extra inch or two compared to a regular full moon. Super moons are they invite you to look at your life, to reveal areas which you usually keep hidden. High in the night sky, they illuminate a great deal of information should you choose to work with this sacred energy. Connecting with this information gives you a fantastic opportunity to expand your life, to reveal areas that are ready to be developed.

As the moon peaks, it naturally begins to wane. As the Moon heads towards the next gravitational shift, the new moon phase, it has a cleansing effect on your emotional awareness. This helps you remove from your life all the things that need to be released, the areas which limit progress said no real good while they are kept within your spirit. Heading into the new Moon gives your excellent opportunity to connect with the mysterious darkness. It is a healing time that brings a powerful sense of cleansing. This removes the outworn energy and makes space for new opportunities to flow into your world as the Moon fills once again into a full shining globe.

PLANETARY RETROGRADES

The Retrograde phase is when a planet appears, when observed from Earth, to reverse direction. This happens due to an optical illusion caused by differences in orbit. The retrograde motion can have a negative influence on your life. The planet Mercury is the best-known planet for retrograde phases. This is because Mercury is the fastest planet in our solar system, and it enters a retrograde motion between three to four times a year, for about three weeks at a time. Mercury is a planet that rules communication, so you can expect frequent misunderstandings, scheduling problems, and disagreements during a Mercury Retrograde phase. Here is a quick reference guide to the retrogrades in 2021.

MERCURY: 3 RETROGRADES IN 2021

VENUS: 1 RETROGRADE IN 2021

MARS: NO RETROGRADE IN 2021

JUPITER: 1 RETROGRADE IN 2021

SATURN: 1 RETROGRADE IN 2021

URANUS: 2 RETROGRADE IN 2021

NEPTUNE: 1 RETROGRADE IN 2021

PLUTO: 1 RETROGRADE IN 2021

NODE: 1 RETROGRADE IN 2021

LILITH: NO RETROGRADE IN 2021

CHIRON: 1 RETROGRADE IN 2021

2021

CAPRICORN HOROSCOPE

Four Weeks Per Month

- Week 1 – Days 1 - 7
- Week 2 – Days 8 - 14
- Week 3 – Days 15 - 21
- Week 4 – Days 22 – Month-end

Time is set to Coordinated Universal Time Zone
(UT±0)

January 3, 4 - Quadrantids Meteor Shower.

The Quadrantids meteor shower run yearly from January 1-5. The Quadrantids meteor shower peaks this year on the night of the 3rd and morning of the 4th.

January 6th – Last Quarter Moon in Libra.

This Moon phase occurs at 09.37 UTC.

January 13th – New Moon in Capricorn.

This new moon phase occurs at 05:02 UTC. This cleans the slate and brings a fresh start. This is an excellent time to view galaxies and stars as there is no moonlight to obscure your view of the universe.

January 20 – First Quarter Moon in Aries.

This Moon phase occurs at 21.02 UTC.

January 24th – Mercury at Greatest Eastern Elongation.

The planet Mercury reaches greatest eastern elongation of 18.6 degrees from the Sun. This occurs at 02.00 UTC. Look for Mercury low in the sky just after sunset.

January 28th - Full Moon in Leo.

This phase occurs at 19:16 UTC. Full Wolf Moon. It has also been known as the Old Moon and the Moon After Yule. The Full Moon illuminates and draws new options to light.

January 29th – Jupiter in Conjunction with the Sun.

The planet Jupiter in Conjunction with the Sun. This occurs at 01:00 UTC.

January 30th – Mercury Retrograde begins in Aquarius.

During a retrograde period, it isn't the right time to move forward in any practical venture. Be prepared for misunderstandings and miscommunications to be prevalent.

The Quadrantids Meteor Shower blazes across the night sky this week. You can set intentions for what you'd like to build over the coming months, your abilities to manifest are on the increase. You are entering a phase of growth, expansion, and heightened potential. As you welcome a surge of inspiration into your world, you embrace a positive aspect which takes you towards developing substantial goals. Now, you find you can broaden your horizons, learn a new area, or even delve into an entrepreneurial idea. Launching your potential is all it takes to realize a long-awaited dream. This may also lead to a breakthrough in your life when a random conversation with another shows promise. You reach a fork in the road where you are required to take a final approach. One path is guiding you towards growth and the learning of skills.

Honing your talents becomes an important theme that stabilizes your life. This is a time of movement and discovery, it leads to a transformation which provides you with many blessings. As you broaden your horizons, you are guided to pay attention to signs which direct your path. The activity is hectic, the pace is forward facing, it is a trailblazing time which sets the stage for some impressive growth. You may find that a lot is going on in your life, it is a time that can feel restless. Positive energy is ready to emerge, taking time to explore the possibilities brings a golden opportunity. Improvements are indicated, this elevates the potential possible. Opportunity is knocking at your door, and paying heed to signs and synchronicity does let the path ahead open wide with refreshing potential.

The New Moon in Capricorn at the week's end brings news. This is a time that helps you be more expressive about what you seek. You don't have to feel guilty about taking the time to develop your own dreams. It is vital to stay motivated and inspired. New options are arriving soon that help peel back the limitations that have been holding you back. It does connect you to a more social environment, and it leads to developing friendships and companions. In taking a step back, you create a sense of empathy that creates a channel toward your dreams. It does let imagination and inspiration flow into your world. A river of new possibilities arrive, and this becomes the gateway from which to grow your abilities. It does bring a long journey that begins with a single step in the right direction. Acknowledging your emotions creates a sacred space that balances and restores your spirit. After a time of soul-searching, your strength and motivation return full force. It does draw rejuvenation, and it provides you with a clean slate. Clearing the path ahead illustrates new possibilities. It does see you revealing an opportunity ahead that connects you with a crew of innovative people. It brings lively discussions and brainstorming sessions. A more social environment lets you thrive. There are some lovely changes ready to flow into your life. They flag a time where you can stop and smell the roses. It does draw an abundant environment that lets you make tracks on developing your personal life. News on the horizon encourages you to walk a path that is in alignment with your heart. This influence reverberates through your life and does connect you with a person who inspires you on every level.

There may be some emotional intensity surrounding your current situation. You can release any uncomfortable feelings, the universe has your back. You are ready to move in alignment with your spirit and listen to the call within your heart. It does build more stable foundations, and this draws abundance into your life. Support is available in your wider community. There are going to be some exciting changes occurring over the coming few weeks. It does erase boundaries and limitations. The path ahead lights up with new possibilities. Perseverance, diligence, and focus let you spot an opportunity that is right for progression. You uncover a hidden gem and reveal a venture that captures your interest. It is soul-affirming and rewarding. Look for signs that offer you a new path. Something is opening soon that begins a new chapter. It does make good use of your practical abilities, and it also provides a more social environment. Conversations ahead get the ball rolling on expanding your life. It does see new energy flowing into your world that is a breath of fresh air. This is the time that draws change into your world. It does bring an option where you can advance your situation forward. Being flexible and paying attention to subtle signs that guide your direction does draw dividends. It is instrumental in progressing the path ahead. An area you focus on does blossom, it brings an expansive chapter of endless possibilities. It gives you the freedom to focus on yourself. It does seem curious news arrives, which provides an exciting path forward. It brings inspiration flowing into your world and lets you set your sights on a lofty goal.

Jupiter goes into Conjunction with the Sun the day after the Full Moon in Leo. Jupiter rules luck, growth, wisdom, and fortune. Life gets a boost from this cosmic alignment, it is a time of releasing the blocks, letting go of areas that no longer have a hold on your awareness. You may feel extra sensitive as your situation is going through some growing pains.

Mercury Retrograde begins in Aquarius at weeks end. There is some conflict surrounding your energy. Addressing what it is that that is unsettling your spirit does create space for healing. You are ready for a new life-cycle, this is an ideal time for releasing the past, healing your emotions, and contemplating the path ahead. In fact, keeping your eyes open, you are likely to spot a new pathway that takes you forward. It does transition you towards a happier chapter. It does seem that you sail to smoother waters. This brings a sense of relief, it lets you feel that you are making progress in life where it is most needed. It builds stable foundations because you are focusing on improving your immediate environment. You can achieve impressive results on the home front. It orients you towards a chapter of movement and discovery. Indeed, it does show that heightened stability is the outcome of being involved with shedding outworn layers. As you peel back areas that are no longer relevant, you break fresh ground and create space for the new potential to blossom. It does seem that secret information is to be revealed soon, this news brings clarity. It lets you see the path ahead more clearly. You find your feet after what has been a destabilizing chapter. The timing is exceptional; it brings an adventure that motivates change.

February 2nd – Imbolc

Harness the element of fire to create something new. Inspiration, motivation, and creativity are rising. The Earth is waking after winter's long sleep.

February 4th – Last Quarter Moon in Scorpio.

This Moon phase occurs at 17.37 UTC.

February 8th – Mercury at Inferior Conjunction.

The planet Mercury at Inferior Conjunction. This occurs at 14:00 UTC.

February 11th - New Moon in Aquarius.

This phase occurs at 19:06 UTC. This is an excellent time to view galaxies and stars as there is no moonlight to obscure your view of the universe. This is a time of rebirth and renewal. Create space for something new to arrive.

February 12th – Chinese New Year (Ox)

February 19 – First Quarter Moon in Taurus.

This Moon phase occurs at 18.47 UTC.

February 21st – Mercury Retrograde ends in Aquarius.

You can now move forward with any delayed plans that you have been putting off due to the Mercury Retrograde phase. Relationships should soon improve as miscommunications are overcome

February 27th - Full Moon in Virgo.

The Moon is on the opposite side of the Earth as the Sun and will be fully illuminated. This phase occurs at 08:17 UTC. This full Moon is known as the Full Snow Moon. Powerful energy lights a path forward. You can attract and manifest excellent results during the complete moon phase.

You face a crossroads soon where you are faced with two choices. It does relate to moving in alignment with your heart so you can move forward with your personal life. You may feel as though you're flying blind, but in actuality, your intuition is guiding this process. It does help you transform the potential possible, and this lets you build better emotional foundations. It brings more stability to your entire life. This is an extraordinary time that creates changes you can in time appreciate. You may be drawn to working on a new venture, and putting in a stamp of individuality on projects as they develop enhances the potential possible. News arrives soon that offers you a chance to dabble in an area of interest. You can bet that life holds an exciting change. It does take you on a journey of new horizons. It speaks of movement and discovery, you can grow and expand your life. It does seem that new things are afoot, and this takes you towards a happy chapter. A willingness to be open to new possibilities helps draw this positive energy into your life. The seeds that are planted during this time do ripen and blossom over the coming chapter. It does bring opportunities for you to be involved in a more social environment. It highlights developing long-held goals and dreams. As you test the waters in fresh territory, you draw new friendships to light. It does bring a sense of connection and abundance to the forefront of your life. It does draw a fruitful time that explores a path that is off the beaten track. It involves seeking an outlet for the excess of creative energy that is burning within your spirit. It is a time that rejuvenates and inspires; you ride a wave of hopeful energy as you shift your focus to a direction that boosts your morale.

The New Moon this week does wipe the slate clean on many levels. Your life has undergone many changes, this can feel unsettling. There is a strong emphasis on improving your experience. An invitation ahead offers a diversion that draws abundance. There is an opportunity to mingle ahead. There is energy simmering, and that brings a foundation in love. Lessons from the past have given you a good sense of flexibility and resourcefulness. It does come in handy and holds you in good stead as there are opportunities ahead to improve your personal life. Life brings a romantic situation forward that lets you build your dreams with another. A new era is coming that sets your heart ablaze with excitement. It takes you towards a fresh slate of potential. There is an exciting element in the air. Life brings opportunities to mingle and engage in lively discussions. Brainstorming sessions occurring within your more full social circle does bring a new possibility into your life. It sees a situation blossoming with someone who sparks your curiosity. Spending time with this individual becomes the gateway from which to grow your social life. It brings expansive horizons and draws harmony into your world. It brings an enjoyable chapter that removes blocks and opens the path ahead. It kicks off a fresh cycle of growth, it does bring new adventures for your social life. It does draw a sweet chapter filled with lively conversation. It brings a heightened sense of well-being and does see a time of personal growth coming into focus. Under this powerful influence, you can achieve an active phase of advancing your dreams.

Mercury Retrograde ends at weeks end. Complications are set to fade, it has been an unsettling time, and there is still a little way to go for things to settle down. It does bring a chance to focus on what is truly meaningful. Taking time to engage in areas that speak to your heart will rebalance and rejuvenate your environment. You get a sense that this is the time that grows your spirit. Something is troubling you and leaving you feeling anxious. As your subconscious situation is in a troubled state, you lean on your friends for support. One, in particular, helps you and provides guidance when you need it the most. This is a time that creates change. The universe supports your growth and evolution. News arrives that is a windfall. You appreciate a lucky break, and it does have you feeling that progress is being made. An area you focus on does move forward. This indicates that limitations are being resolved, it helps you take advantage of a fresh flow of energy that breaks up outworn areas. This gets the fires of inspiration burning brightly in your life. It is the perfect time to set the scene of emerging abundance that is around the corner for you. It does create an ideal link between your goals and future vision. It bodes well for getting involved in a more social environment that heightens the potential in your life. It does bring communication, there is a discussion ahead that lets you appreciate the blessings that surround your life. It does strengthen ties and deepens a bond you value. It brings the sunshine into your life. An opportunity comes knocking that sees potential blossoming. It does bring a breakthrough that is a turning point. It speaks about new horizons, something curious is coming provides you with a path you can embrace.

The Full Moon in Virgo occurs this week, this can create energy peaks that illuminate and draw clarity. It is a time of generating leads and mapping out the finer details for a journey of growth. You are on the precipice of dramatic change, it touches all areas of your life. It re-establishes you in a more settled and productive environment. There may be a difficult decision ahead that helps you move away from areas that are no longer relevant or helpful. Taking a leap of faith, you begin a journey that is evolving and guiding you towards heightened potential. An attractive option emerges from the mist to tempt you forward. The path ahead opens when you get back in touch with your long-term goals. You make adjustments and begin a chapter that correlates with improving your immediate environment. Smart decisions are made that stack up nicely. They take you towards an optimistic time of goal setting and planning. You are ready to evolve and bring something new to light. Information is coming, and that shines a light on a curious path forward. Changes in the air, a fresh wind of potential arrives to bring new possibilities to your life. It does let you build a foundation that is stable and secure. You reach for your dreams and reveal a path of exciting adventures awaits your open heart. This journey offers a remarkable chance to heal the past and restore faith to your spirit. It brings abundance into focus as a sense of joy fills your view. You discover a path that tempts you forward, it does bring a fast-moving environment that enables you to adapt and maintain flexibility over the coming chapter. It brings new options; you are ready to raise the bar and pursue your vision.

March 6th - Mercury Greatest Elongation.

The planet Mercury reaches its greatest elongation of 27.3 degrees from the Sun. If you would like to view Mercury, look for Mercury low in the eastern sky just before sunrise.

March 6th – Last Quarter Moon in Sagittarius.

This Moon phase occurs at 01.30 UTC. –

March 11th – Neptune in Conjunction with the Sun.

The planet Neptune in Conjunction with the Sun. This occurs at 00:00 UTC.

March 13th - New Moon in Pisces.

The New Moon creates space for a new chapter. This phase occurs at 10:21 UTC. This is an excellent time to observe galaxies and stars because there is no moonlight to obscure your view of the universe.

March 20th - Vernal Equinox.

The March equinox takes place at 09:37 UTC. There are equal amounts of day and night throughout the world.

March 21 – First Quarter Moon in Gemini.

This Moon phase occurs at 14.40 UTC.

March 26th - Venus Superior Conjunction.

The planet Venus at Superior Conjunction. This occurs at 06:00 UTC.

March 28th - Full Moon in Libra.

This Moon is on the opposite side of the Earth as the Sun and shall be fully illuminated. This phase occurs at 18:48 UTC. This full Moon is known as the Full Worm Moon. Powerful energy lights a path forward. You can attract and manifest excellent results during the complete moon phase.

Mercury reaches greatest elongation this week. This can feel destabilizing, but in fact, it creates a useful change, you move away from destructive influences and create lifestyle changes that draw benefits. The information arrives that takes a moment to digest. It does bring an opportunity that supports a stable phase of growth. It is time that sees you becoming quite busy. Events play out in your favor when you are allowed to grow your world. An offer lands at your feet. It does add up to a productive and lively environment. You see changes around your life that offer a sense of progression and growth.

All in all, this improves the stability of the home front. It does give you more options and places you in the box seat to expand your life into a new area. You enter a happy chapter that brings new changes. There are adjustments made that define the path and create a smoother environment. This brings you an opportunity to advance a personal goal. There is a strong emphasis on communication ahead. It does have you thinking about the possibilities. A unique aspect is coming, and that brings out secrets and hidden information. It does highlight a journey towards heightened communication with an individual of interest. Getting to know this person's entire back history does let you see them with a new perspective. It is a favorable time to develop a bond of the heart. News arrives from someone who has been thinking about you recently. This gets you back on track and leaves you feeling inspired. This is a time that lights up pathways of creativity and self-expression. It does bring an exciting adventure that captures the essence of freedom and liberation.

Neptune arrives in conjunction with the Sun this week. The Planet Neptune rules dreams and healing, while the Sun places a strong focus on self-development. The influence of the Sun draws an energizing power that bolsters your spirit. Ideas, insight, and inspiration weave magic and help you manifest a path towards your dreams. It does see delays are no longer likely to hinder your progress. Things are on the move again, this gets you back in the saddle and lets you hit your stride. Being open to fresh possibilities heightens the outcomes possible. Be flexible and prepared to change directions. Events on the horizon may compel you to try a new path. It does highlight a time of freedom and adventure that places a strong emphasis on developing your higher creative vision. It brings a turning point, a time that rules a blend of artistic inspiration. A new project ahead hits the ticket for drawing blessings into your world. It does light a favorable path forward. You can initiate something new over the coming weeks. It does see the fires of your creativity are stirring and reconnecting you to ideas and inspiration. It helps you break away from old patterns and pick up leads that bring new possibilities into your life. The time ahead is a lucky phase of expansion. It does rule advancing an area that inspires your mind. Consistency is the key that takes you to a successful outcome. A unique option is coming that gives you a chance to grow a dream. It does have you on a mission to advance and progress an area of importance. This focus is very healing as it gives you a welcome boost that shifts you forward. It comes at a delicate time and lets you make the most of a positive chapter.

Ostara, the Spring Equinox, takes center stage this week. It's all about facing the sun again after the long winter and starting new plans and goals, you can harvest later in the year. This is a great time to clear the decks and keep open to new possibilities. An ending arrives that may make you feel nostalgic or sentimental. It does bring adjustments as you transition to a new chapter. Staying flexible allows you to transition forward smoothly. The path lights up with new potential, you soon leave regret behind and make waves on chasing a unique aspect. Your intuition sparks imagination, expression, and creativity. You score a chance to grow your abilities. It represents a fluid and flexible environment where adaptability is vital. Your internal guidance system helps point you in the right direction and navigate the path ahead adeptly. You open a new way. Your life changes, and it does seem a new possibility crop up, which pleasantly aligns you. This direction does bring growth. You enter a prosperous phase where you can rise above the challenges and explore unleashing your capabilities into new areas. It sees you heading towards a perfect place; your optimism draws dividends. Several cross-currents are flowing through your life, and this can cause confusion. Being actively involved in clearing the path does bring clarity. You can be proactive about moving forward as you climb the ladder towards abundance. Sowing seeds and nurturing their growth leads to an active phase of growth. Specific goals you put in place do unfold, and this heartens your spirit. It does begin a fascinating chapter that offers unique pathways to growth.

Venus sashays into your life this week, it is a time that draws fulfillment. An impromptu social event provides you with a remarkable opportunity, it sets the stage for future get-togethers with someone who inspires your mind. You are in the process of setting the tone for a new cycle of growth. It lets you generate an original path that draws excitement. It puts you in contact with others who elevate your vision by inspiring you to think big and chase those dreams. A buzz of excitement soon reveals a path that takes you further. It brings curious talks about draw social invitations ahead. It does draw tranquility and leaves you feeling content.

Additionally, the Full Moon in Libra highlights a time of increasing opportunity, a major makeover is coming. The path ahead brings such lovely news. You catch a winning project. This assignment enables you to develop your talents. It does release the tension and brings exciting possibilities to build a new role. New foundations are coming for you soon. In has a positive aspect that wipes the slate clean. It does take a little longer than expected to come together. It brings a momentous time for building a stable environment. Which ultimately, improves your circumstances. Good news is ahead, and this brings the stellar chapter where you can make progress on your vision. An impending breakthrough is coming. You can have faith that your idea holds water. It takes strength and perseverance, as it has been a confusing time. You move towards finishing up details on achieving this goal. It brings many side projects, but the wheels are in motion. There is someone close to you who is of assistance collaboratively. This person is quite helpful when you need it the most.

April 4th – Last Quarter Moon in Capricorn.

This Moon phase occurs at 10.02 UTC.

April 12th - New Moon in Aries.

The New Moon phase occurs at 2:31 UTC. This is an excellent time to observe galaxies and stars because there is no moonlight visible.

April 19th – Mercury at Superior Conjunction.

The planet Mercury at Superior Conjunction. This occurs at 02:00 UTC.

April 20 – First Quarter Moon in Leo.

This Moon phase occurs at 06.59 UTC.

April 22, 23 - Lyrids Meteor Shower.

The Lyrids meteor shower runs each year from April 16-25. This meteor shower peaks on the night of the 22nd and the morning of the 23rd. These meteors can produce bright dust trails that last for several seconds.

April 27th - Full Moon in Scorpio, Supermoon.

The Moon is on the opposite side of the Earth as the Sun and will be completely illuminated. Full Pink Moon. It's the first of three supermoons for 2021. This occurs at 03:31 UTC. The Moon will be at its closest approach to the Earth and may look slightly larger and brighter than usual. Powerful energy lights a path forward. You can attract and manifest excellent results during the full moon phase.

April 30th – Uranus in Conjunction with the Sun.

The planet Uranus in Conjunction with the Sun. This occurs at 21:00 UTC.

It seems there an area of your life wrapped in mist. News ahead unlocks information, and clarity is gained. It does clear the path and lets you move away from a problematic area. Finding the correct solution essentially dissolves hold-ups. It opens a door that until recently had been closed. It brings new potential, and the wheels turn in your favor. It brings a growth-orientated chapter that enables you to progress your journey forward.

You may feel unsettled as it has been an unpredictable time, careful consideration does lay a framework that brings stability into focus. An opportunity on the horizon has you feeling more grounded. It does seem refreshing options are highlighted for you soon. You may have been dealing with the healing aspect, and revisiting the past does close the problematic book chapter. It washes away, outworn energy, and creates space for you to move forward. Most of all, reconnecting with your more full social circle is likely to draw dividends. Your willingness to persevere and explore new possibilities does draw profits. You discover the path ahead suddenly clears. It does bring change on a personal and private level. You feel enlightened when a floodlight of clarity flows into your life. It does bring news about developing a bond that offers room to grow into something truly spectacular. You focus your energy on an area that inspires your heart. It is a time that lets you make progress. It opens doors and does help you uncover a path towards developing an area of interest. This is good news for your life, it brings a positive aspect that sees you glowing. It sees you rise to the occasion and fling open a new chapter.

The New Moon in Aries packs a nugget of wisdom. It is a time of excitement and creativity, it does have you dreaming big about future goals. Inspiration brings ideas that provide workable solutions to any given situation. It does help you make snap decisions that grow the potential possible in your world. It does bring a time that has you overseeing new responsibilities. Some challenges see you rising to meet your goals head-on. You can be confident that things will work out as you have built a reasonable basis of lessons learned from previous chapters.

A more social environment ahead that lets you participate in discussions that generate a wide variety of solutions. It does bring new leads to feed your hungry mind. It triggers a unique journey that enables you to grow an interest you've had on the backburner for a while. There may be a collaboration that takes this project further. It does bring an aspect of growth that may have you involved in developing a new path. This is a time that offers new possibilities to grow your situation. It does see an area that you nurture being compatible with growth. It brings a new strategy that lets you embrace a fast-moving and more active environment. It draws the perfect conditions to dive into a chapter that is freedom-loving and expansive. It activates a social element that brings a change of scene. News arrives that is worth its weight in gold. It does bring a remedy that has you surrounded by friends and companions. It brings a more social element that offers you room to spread your wings and take your vision higher. It brings a compatible time that provides an ideal sense of connection. Getting involved in a group environment hits a sweet soft spot for your spirit.

Mercury at Superior conjunction this week sees you reaching a crossroads. It is a time that may test your patience and demand more of your emotional reserves. If you have been going through a healing process, know that it does lead to change, progress, and productivity. It is a dramatic tool that creates space to clear the path ahead. News arrives that offers a message of hope. It does see a shift forward that culminates in a series of advantageous moments. It marks a significant turning point. It does bring more emotional energy into your life. A bond of friendship emerges that touches your heart. It brings a path of developing your hopes and wishes. This highlights an opportunity to join a group or situation that produces a lovely friendship. It ushers in new possibilities for your social life and lets you move in a positive direction. Taking time to create a stable emotional base does draw dividends. It does allow you to take advantage of opportunities that spring up to tempt you forward. Something impressive is coming, it takes time to land, so be patient. It positions you in an ideal alignment to advance an innovative goal. This helps you create changes that offer room to stretch your abilities into new areas. You seal the deal by being open and flexible to new pathways. Releasing the tension and your troubles do wipe the slate clean. It gives the universe a clear indication that you are ready for new friendships and companions. You may discover a group environment that hits the ticket to a more connected environment. You have lovely talents you can nurture through getting involved with developing your abilities. Cutting the cord of the past brings an open road of adventure ahead that is a saving grace.

The Full Moon in Scorpio is a Supermoon that sweeps into your life to draw closure, healing, and this transitions you forward. A more vibrant life experience arrives to heal an aspect that has been out of alignment recently. It does help you release bottled up emotions that have caused tension that limited your true potential. It underscores an atmosphere of acceptance that brings balance and lets you built new foundations. It keeps you in touch with possibilities that take you towards freedom and expansion. It generates a fresh start. You are moving in a robust and positive direction. It does see new opportunities being created that take you towards an active time. Prosperity is coming that helps you launch a new chapter. Good fortune sees life sparkling with excitement ahead. It does bring an expansive social environment that triggers new friendships. You create magic through your willingness to be open to change. Adjustments ahead refine the potential possible in your world. It does culminate in a succession of opportunities that arrive are much like the rungs of the ladder. As you climb upward, you get a broader view of the potential possible. Growing your talents brings you towards a phase that triggers essential life events. It does bring a busy time for building your environment. Your life has been shaken up, you can now let the dust settle and resume moving forward in due course. It does seem new possibilities are coming that tempt you towards a chapter of expansion. It provides better conditions to grow your life, it brings a sense of adventure and inspiration into play that helps you start a new chapter. It reminds you of your passion for life and reconnects you with your creativity

May 3rd – Last Quarter Moon in Aquarius.

This Moon phase occurs at 17.50 UTC.

May 6, 7 - Eta Aquarids Meteor Shower.

The Eta Aquarids meteor shower runs annually from April 19th to May 28th. It peaks this year on the night of May 6th and the morning of May 7th.

May 11th - New Moon in Taurus.

This phase occurs at 19:00 UTC. The new moon phase is a brilliant time to observe galaxies and stars because there is no moonlight visible.

March 17th - Mercury Greatest Eastern Elongation.

The planet Mercury reaches its greatest eastern elongation of 22 degrees from the Sun. If you would like to view Mercury, look for the Mercury low in the sky just after sunset. This planetary phase occurs at 06.00 UTC.

May 19 – First Quarter Moon in Virgo.

This Moon phase occurs at 19.13 UTC.

May 26th - Full Moon in Sagittarius, Supermoon.

This phase occurs at 11:14 UTC. Full Flower Moon. It's the second of three supermoons for 2021. The Moon will be at its closest approach to the Earth and may look slightly larger and brighter than usual. Powerful energy lights a path forward. You can attract and manifest excellent results during the full moon phase.

May 26th – A Total Lunar Eclipse in Sagittarius.

A total lunar eclipse occurs when the Moon passes completely through the Earth's dark shadow or umbra. During this type of eclipse, the Moon gradually gets more mysterious and then take on a rusty or blood red color. This eclipse occurs at 11:19 UTC.

May 29th – Mercury Retrograde begins in Gemini.

During a retrograde period, it isn't the right time to move forward in any practical venture. Be prepared for misunderstandings and miscommunications to be prevalent.

Focusing on the essentials takes moves you forward, there is a goal you develop that helps to establish yourself in a new area. It is perfect for growing your talent. You enter a new role that connects you with new friends and goals. It does bring improvements that can be rapid, and the environment is active and productive. All told, it has you moving forward towards a happy chapter. It speaks about new options arriving that tempt you towards growth. It explicitly highlights the information that comes for you soon. It lets you gain traction on developing a broader vision and puts you in the box seat to improve your life through a series of expansive moves. It ignites new energy that kicks off an exciting chapter. Life becomes brighter when green pastures beckon and tempt you forward. There are rewards to be had by exploring new possibilities. It does ramp potential up to a higher level. A celebration ahead sees festivities ruling, and this leads to a more vibrant and social environment to dip your toes into. It does bring opportunities to discuss ideas and bond with others. A heart-to-heart conversation opens the door on a new chapter of connection. It does take you to an exciting phase where you share discussions and ideas with someone who holds meaning to you. It sets the scene for a lively and adventurous chapter to follow. It is a time of change; you discover a crossroads that has you thinking about the past, and the intersection ahead brings a turning point. It does mark a time of shifting your focus forward, drawing new options to light that creates space for a bold new beginning.

The Taurus New Moon this week speaks of the change that arrives on a personal and societal level. It does enlighten your life with new possibilities. The timing is fortuitous, it brings an open road to explore. An original source of inspiration is coming that sparks the fires of creativity. It does let you scope out an area that offers room to progress your talents. You can continue to press on towards your goals and know that you are supported by the stars above. It is a time that brings an ending, and within a short space, it lets a new beginning usher into your life. Keeping your eyes open, you spot a path that lets you travel lightly forward towards further growth. It does highlight the way of security and stability. It brings a sense of connection that enables you to tap into your more full social environment. Any issues that are on the periphery are soon sidelined and put behind you. Someone in your more full social circle has been keeping their thoughts close to their chest. There is a secret that is likely to be revealed soon. It does bring a new source of inspiration into your life when this person overcomes the shyness and gets real about sharing their thoughts with you. Signs ahead show a positive outlook is on the horizon. A bond of companionship is deepened through transparent communication. It delivers an upbeat time that sees life moving faster. It does bring good news, it's has you celebrating with a broader group of friends. It does introduce you to some new contacts. The path suddenly clicks open; this helps you zoom towards new possibilities. It brings a prosperous time for social expansion, and there is a high lift coming to your personal life that is quite refreshing.

Mercury reaches greatest elongation from the Sun this week. Your strength and vitality are returning, it does seem life force energy is flowing into your life to instigate the return of expansion. Opportunities to mingle are coming, new friends and companions arrive to set the stage for a lively chapter of interpersonal interaction. There is positive communication ahead that bring new ideas to light. It does have you exploring a path that offers room to grow into a passion project. It speaks about a positive trend that is coming. It does bring opportunities to socialize, exploring new ideas stimulates your creativity and brings you the motivation to experiment with a variety of pathways. There is an outlet that nurtures your spirit and draws abundance into your life. It will be a strong focus for you over the coming chapter. It does seem you turn a corner and head towards adventure. A wave of opportunities arrives for you soon. It does see decisions being made; plans been tweaked as life proceeds towards expansion. It does touch a social aspect that has you mingling with like-minded people. It brings projects and endeavors that inspire you creatively. As you settle into a new path, you get a practical idea of what can be achieved when you put your mind to it. Life picks up the pace soon when a whirlwind of activity arrives to inspire your soul. It does bring a flow of positive energy as things begin to shift forward. There is terrific stability on offer, you can reap the rewards from your willingness to expand horizons and grow new areas. It all helps remove the heaviness that has cloaked your life recently. It brings a lighter, more lively chapter ahead.

This week delivers a plethora of cosmic activity. There is a full moon in Sagittarius, which is also a super moon, and on the same night, a total lunar eclipse. This is a triple magnifying event. Three days later, Mercury retrograde begins in Gemini. This is the mule kick that may just knock you sideways if you're not aware that it is coming. So what does all this mean for your life? The triple combo event on Wednesday brings changes that spark a new path.

Furthermore, during a Mercury Retrograde phase, you are best to do your own thing and not be drawn into any drama. It seems you are on a trajectory that is diverging from what you truly seek. It does take you to a time where you say enough is enough, and you move in alignment with your heart. It does bring a time of contemplation that asks you to make the difficult decisions necessary to live the life you deserve. It seems some boundaries need re-establishing, outstanding bonds to be balanced. As you set the bar higher, you draw the right opportunities into your life. It does seem that recently someone has hidden information from you. Something comes out casually or is discovered by surprise. It brings clarity and gives you insight into the path ahead. It clears the air, and if there has been a miscommunication occurring with a loved one, it does bring a time of re-establishing more stable foundations. Setting boundaries helps minimize the drama in your life. It enables you to ground your energy and stabilize your foundations. There is a silver lining that emerges from doing this work. Restocking your emotional bank does cause a profound psychological shift, it also enables the potential to flow into your life.

JUNE ASTROLOGY

June 2nd – Last Quarter Moon in Pisces.

This Moon phase occurs at 07.24 UTC.

June 10th - New Moon in Gemini.

This moon phase occurs at 10:53 UTC. This is an excellent time to observe galaxies and stars because there is little moonlight to obstruct your view.

June 10th – A Annual Solar Eclipse.

An annular solar eclipse occurs when the Moon is too far away from the Earth to completely cover the Sun, it results in a ring of light around the dark Moon. The Sun's corona isn't visible during an annular eclipse. This solar eclipse is visible in eastern Russia, the Arctic Ocean, western Greenland, and Canada. A partial eclipse will be visible in the northeastern United States, Europe, and most of Russia. This eclipse occurs at 10.42 UTC.

June 11th – Mercury at Inferior Conjunction.

The planet Mercury at Inferior Conjunction. This occurs at 01:00 UTC.

June 18 – First Quarter Moon in Libra.

This Moon phase occurs at 03.54 UTC.

June 21st - June Solstice.

The June solstice occurs at 03:32 UTC. The North Pole will be tilted toward the Sun, which, having reached its northernmost position in the sky, will be over the Tropic of Cancer at 23.44 degrees north latitude. This heralds the first day of summer (summer solstice) in the Northern Hemisphere, the summer solstice is considered one of the most important times of the year for many traditional cultures.

June 22nd – Mercury Retrograde ends in Gemini.

You can now move forward with any delayed plans that you have been putting off due to the Mercury Retrograde phase. Relationships should soon improve as miscommunications are overcome

June 24th - Full Moon in Capricorn, Supermoon.

The Moons will be completely illuminated. This moon phase occurs at 18:40 UTC. Full Strawberry Moon. This is the last of three supermoons for 2021. The Moon will be at its closest approach to the Earth and may look slightly larger and brighter than usual. Powerful energy lights a path forward. You can attract and manifest excellent results during the full moon phase.

You have the stamina to stay on top of things during this Mercury Retrograde phase. It does see you performing at a heightened level, and this brings an offer ahead. It gives you a chance to flex your abilities and create a new start in an area of interest. Your potential moves forward in leaps and bounds. This is the time that rules expansion, you may find your emotions run high with inspiration. Discovering a path that opens by surprise is a saving grace that blends creativity beautifully with your aspirations. It does help you negotiate what has been a tricky environment and move forward towards calmer waters. Staying flexible provides you with plenty of opportunities to explore. As you progress in alignment with your soul, you can look forward to a refreshing change of pace. Overcoming challenges reward you with strength. It does bring a sense of purpose that enables you to investigate new leads and learn skills that capitalize on your talents in the highest way possible. This is the time that may demand change, and this can have you feeling unsettled. You do reveal a diamond in the rough over the coming weeks. It brings a surprise that draws progress. It pulls you out of your usual routine and challenges you to set the bar higher as you grow your abilities. A new chapter brings a fresh start. It does offer a path that draws security. Pacing yourself, prioritizing, and focusing on areas that hold the highest meaning hold you in good stead to handle a more active pace ahead. It does bring a new chapter, you are set to enter a happier phase, and this brings new possibilities to explore. Life becomes more settled and efficient, it does seem that good news is coming soon, sunny skies light the way forward.

The New Moon in Gemini combines with an annular solar eclipse. Focusing your energy on home life does build a stable and secure foundation. You enter a time that is ruled by seeing friends and being in your community. It is a breath of fresh air, it launches an active phase of social expansion that draws abundance. You generate your own luck and magic during this expressive time. It does bode well for your life as it brings sunshine into your world. It is a productive and active environment that offers room to explore all that life has to offer. Soon doors begin to open up. It does bring a wave of exciting potential into your life. If you have found that you have had to keep your guard up and be healthy, new possibilities let you leave the tension behind. It does bring luck and fortune into your circumstances. You may also discover that the past comes calling and reconnects you with someone of interest. You enter new territory soon. It does light up information that comes as a surprise. There may be someone who has been concealing a secret, and this is revealed. It could change your view about this person and explain an aspect that is currently unknown. Having the full story does let you make an informed decision. You discover the road ahead is opening bringing news. A secret is revealed that cracks open new potential with someone in your broader social environment. This person has been trying to ignore a yearning to open their thoughts with you. There is an opportunity ahead to discuss things on a deeper level, it does bring secret personal news. Understanding how this person is thinking opens a new path, and it brings you an opportunity to deepen the bond.

The June 21st Solstice at weeks end is an ideal time to reflect on your goals. It is a time that can feel difficult, but it does instigate growth and change. In can transform your potential and let you explore new pathways that have many lessons to teach you. Pearls of wisdom are sent into your life and help shape the path forward. It does bring a new level of being that soon settles you into an abundant landscape. It's a time where decisions shape destiny. You may find there are two paths open to you, and you need to pause and contemplate the road ahead. Choosing a direction that is in alignment with your heart does bring a journey that resonates positively in your life. It illuminates the brilliant potential that is coming into your life, it does bring considerable personal growth. This transition lets you move forward away from all that is no longer relevant. This is the time that creates change, you may have to get used to experiencing life differently. It does bring personal growth into your life. You can build a bridge forward towards a happy and secure chapter. Taking time to rebalance your energy is highly rejuvenating, it creates a strong basis from which to grow your life. A more social environment soon beckons and draws a new friendship to light. As you settle into a new normal, you discover growth arrives in unexpected ways. It does stir up the winds of change, and this takes you towards a positive chapter. It brings opportunities to socialize with kindred spirits. There is a new chapter opening in your social life, and this highlights an expansive time where you connect with other like-minded individuals. Communication is highlighted as being especially strong.

Mercury Retrograde ends this week. If you have been feeling disconnected or restless recently, it is a time for restoring balance in your world. Being adaptable and flexible does bring the most excellent variety of leads. New information is coming that reveals a path forward. Growth and learning create a strong foundation, a course or necessary instruction is indicated for this new role. It does open the book on a new chapter, this position offers added responsibilities, and there is room for progression over time. It does seem a leadership role is ahead. Indeed, it will seem like you've opened a window and let the fresh air in. A new flow of potential is refreshing and rejuvenate your spirit. It is a balm for your soul, and it brings the creativity back into your full world force. You begin to focus on projects and endeavors that inspire your passion. You discover that you can slowly build a foundation that is forged in titanium and rock-solid. It is a time that brings communication, you find out a bond that is nurtured can develop further. It effectively brings new potential to your l life. You crack open a chapter that inspires growth and lets you move forward towards setting a particular goal. A cluster of social activity is coming that helps create a hotspot of potential. Spending time in a group environment does bring a chance to mingle. You discover a bond with the one who supports your life, this person changes the way you think about the future. It does bring active discussions that have you planning for the future.

JULY ASTROLOGY

July 1st – Last Quarter Moon in Aries.

This Moon phase occurs at 21.11 UTC.

July 4th - Mercury at Greatest Western Elongation.

The planet Mercury reaches greatest western elongation of 20.6 degrees from the Sun. If you would like to view Mercury, look for Mercury low in the eastern sky just before sunrise. This planetary phase occurs at 20.00 UTC.

July 10th - New Moon in Cancer.

The New Moon draws rebirth and new energy. This moon phase occurs at 01:17 UTC. This is an excellent time to observe galaxies and stars because there is no moonlight visible.

July 17 – First Quarter Moon in Libra.

This Moon phase occurs at 10.11 UTC.

July 24th - Full Moon in Aquarius.

The Moon is located on the opposite side of the Earth as the Sun and will be fully illuminated. This phase occurs at 02:37 UTC. This full Moon is known as Full Buck Moon. Powerful energy lights a path forward. You can attract and manifest excellent results during the complete moon phase.

July 28, 29 - Delta Aquarids Meteor Shower.

The Delta Aquarids meteor shower peaks on the night of July 28th and the morning of July 29th. The first quarter moon may block many of the fainter meteors this year. You should still be able to view some brighter ones. Best views should occur after midnight. Meteors radiate from the constellation Aquarius but may appear anywhere in the sky.

July 31st – Last Quarter Moon in Taurus.

This Moon phase occurs at 13.16 UTC.

Mercury at Greatest elongation this week brings unique vibrations. While this is a time that puts roadblocks in your way, but you can overcome obstacles and refine your outlook. Setting appropriate boundaries does remove the drama. It enables you to build foundations that are stable and secure. In fact, a new phase is ready to be launched, this is something that takes you towards a compatible area of interest. It does let you grow creatively and give you the energy that motivates you to learn a skill and refine your talents. The good news is coming. This opportunity will take your full attention, do see something important coming that enriches your life. It brings a social environment that puts you in contact with friends and family. It is a happy development, things are moving forward. This nurtures your spirit and draws an abundant chapter of developing bonds with loved ones. A new chapter that has you working on improving security and stability. It offers a firm and robust basis from which to grow your life. A dream is explored and nurtured. This project becomes a vital aspect that releases stress, it lets you feel excited about developing your goals. Planning and strategy play an important part that takes you towards success. Power and strength arrive to deliver a boost. If you have found your energy flagging recently, this brings inspiration, which leads to a productive environment. Simplicity, at its essence, is a significant contributor to drawing stabilizing energy during this particular time. It also underscores a willingness to adapt and remain flexible, opening your heart to new pathways does bring creative solutions.

The New Moon in Cancer this week signifies a new beginning. You enter a time where your accomplishments receive recognition. It helps you capitalize on your talents and puts your best qualities in the spotlight, you discover a door opens towards developing an area of interest. It brings a busy time that puts the focus on building security. A milestone ahead brings a vital turning point. It takes your skills to a new level. Evolution is essential and brings essential changes. Expanding your horizons lands you in the lap of freedom and adventure. It eclipses anything you've known before. It delivers excellent opportunities to dive in and explore new territory. Working on developing this project is likely to turn into quite a passion for you. It does encourage you to be a pathfinder and uncover little nuggets of gold worth exploring. It progresses your life and introduces you to environments that are enriching.

Furthermore, the time will soon be right to expand your social circle. It does see a return of optimism, vigor, drive, and purpose. It helps you clear the decks and make way for new possibilities to light a path forward. There is a necessary transition occurring, which is a process of healing and acceptance. It does facilitate moving your energy forward towards a happier phase. It is a time that reveals secret information. It does show news arrives that brings a refreshing discovery. Personal developments come to the forefront of your life. It does see you make notable tracks on developing a bond of the heart. Restrictive patterns are released, and this lets you plot a course for future growth. It involves a leap of faith. It takes you towards a bountiful chapter of open communication with another.

It is an unsettling time where many rapid changes can leave you feeling frazzled. You may feel especially receptive to vibrations of the past. It brings a river of compassion and empathy into your surroundings. If you feel pulled in many directions, taking time to pause and restock your spirit does bring grounding energy that helps you fortify your foundations. Feeling nostalgic is part of this process, and lets you process emotions. It takes you towards healing and creates space for the new potential to emerge soon after. Letting go of past baggage lets, you release unresolved feelings. You shut the door on an area that is best moved away from. It does set your energy free and helps you move forward towards greener pastures. You enter a time that sees improvement flowing into your world. It does have an especially beneficial impact on your spirit. It helps you release emotional blockages that have previously been anchored in anxiety. Releasing this tension does ground your mind. It brings personal growth and takes you towards an environment that is dynamic, happy, and abundant. As you build a new phase of your own foundations, you set the stage for progress. It does create space for new potential, a fresh outlook draws dividends. Life becomes more peaceful when you explore the potential that expands your life with exciting possibilities. It is time that connects you to magic and opportunity. It relates to interpersonal bonds and developing social ties. The nurturing you give to others is returned back into your life. A new avenue opens, and this brings opportunities to mingle, it helps you build a deeper level of connection with someone who is connected to you on an emotional level.

The magic of the Full Moon arrives to put you in a contemplative mode. Nurturing your environment is essential, you can focus on areas that heal your spirit, a vision of the past may impact you significantly during this time. A vital transition ahead connects you with new possibilities. It restores and rejuvenates. You enter a time of heightened creativity that brings a journey you can appreciate. It lets you forge a compelling path forward that revolutionizes the potential possible in your world. It is a journey of self-discovery that enriches your spirit and places you in the box seat to discover a new friend. There is a focus on improving your emotional base.

Expect new friendships to arrive that tempt you to explore new directions. The path ahead clears, and it reveals a bevy of exciting possibilities. It does bring a new chapter that lets you shift your focus forward. An appealing option emerges that opens a gateway towards an exciting path of developing a dream you hold dear. You harness the pioneering aspect and blaze a trail forward toward your vision. It does bring leads that inspire your mind as it carries the essence of manifestation on the winds of change. It brings new possibilities to your life that let you tap into a broader arena of potential. It's a time that marks a transition forward. It does help you grow your wild ambitions, and this brings fuel to your inspiration. News arrives soon, which is a boost to your spirit. You soon awaken to a sense of abundance that gives you the information needed to move forward.

August 1st – Mercury at Superior Conjunction.

The planet Mercury at Superior Conjunction. This planetary event occurs at 14:00 UTC.

August 2nd - Saturn at Opposition.

The beautiful ringed planet Saturn will be at its nearest approach to Earth and will be illuminated by the Sun. This planetary event occurs at 05:00 UTC.

August 8th - New Moon in Leo.

This moon phase occurs at 13:50 UTC. This is an excellent time to observe galaxies and stars because there is no moonlight to obstruct the view. A new chapter awaits an open heart.

August 12, 13 - Perseids Meteor Shower.

The Perseids meteor shower runs each year from July 17th to August 24th. It peaks this year on the night of August 12th and the morning of August 13th. The Perseids meteor shower is usually excellent viewing as the meteors are so bright and numerous. The Moon sets early in the evening, leaving dark skies for what could be a unique show. The best viewing is from after midnight.

August 15 – First Quarter Moon in Scorpio.

This Moon phase occurs at 15.20 UTC.

August 19th - Jupiter at Opposition.

The Giant planet Jupiter will be at its nearest approach to Earth and will be at it's brightest. This planetary event occurs at 23:00 UTC.

August 22nd - Full Moon in Aquarius, Blue Moon.

The Full Moon draws clarity and illumination. This phase occurs at 12:02 UTC. Full Sturgeon Moon. This year it is also a blue moon. This event only happens on average once every 2.7 years, giving rise to the term, "once in a blue moon." There are three full moons in each season of the year. But as full moons occur every 29.53 days, occasionally a season contains 4 full moons. The additional full Moon of the season is known as a blue moon.

August 30th – Last Quarter Moon in Gemini.

This Moon phase occurs at 07.13 UTC.

Saturn at opposition this week brings the energy that is diligent, persevering, reliable, stable, patient. You see life with a fresh perspective, it does release the anxiety. It is soothing, this is sustenance to your spirit. It brings a gift of expansion, activity, and growth. A productive and active cycle soon tempts you forward. It brings a target you can aim for. A touch of magic surrounds the changes ahead. In a short while, you hit upon a time of celebration that impacts your life favorably. It does bring opportunities to mingle, it increases your social circle and adds a dash of excitement. These changes nourish your environment and provide you with the right ingredients to blend social connection with interpersonal communication. Spending time with a lively crew draws abundance. It does unlock a chapter that enables you to transform your world by being open to change. A happy section ahead brings new possibilities into your life. It sees you collaborating with others of a similar mindset. There is communication with the valuable mentors who give you guidance and enable you to trust you are progressing the direction ahead correctly. It is a time of growth and personal initiatives that draw happiness. You enter a time of change that sweeps away negativity. This releases the blockages that have limited your life recently. It places you in alignment with the direction that grows your world. It draws a lovely time that brings enriching experiences and good fortune. A new page opens in your book of life, it has you initiating a path that inspires your mind. A fresh approach brings a new initiative; it gives you a time of growth.

The New Moon in Leo this week delivers good fortune with a flurry of excitement. It does see things shift and lighten. A tempting offer comes that breathes fresh air into your surroundings. Things are on the move, change is swirling around your life. It does draw new pathways that take you towards growth. Being open to new possibilities does kick off a cycle of good fortune. It marks an exciting time that lets you make exceptional progress in developing your goals. You can set your sights high. Opportunity arrives and brings optimism to the winds of change. There is a focus on self-development that gets you involved in learning new methods and developing your talents. It positions you in alignment with improving a journey that is close to your heart. You discover you can grow your life in many beautiful ways. This creates a bridge towards a brighter chapter. It marks the start of something big, a phase that is vibrant and fun. A new beginning arrives that breathes fresh air into your surroundings. It is the shift forward you have been seeking. It provides a new cycle of growth where you can accomplish a great deal by being open to new adventures. Life supports a journey that expands your social circle. It does put you on the right path to mingle with new friends. There is a unique and original journey on offer that is specifically designed to advance your life. It brings an auspicious chapter that enables you to transform your world by removing areas that limit progress. Focusing on a path that offers room to develop your personal vision does bring a vital phase of growth.

There is a restless vibe that can feel disconcerting, it does bring change. Still, you can adjust to a fast-moving environment with the right mindset. The past has been a journey of growth and change. You may feel sentimental at this time as you are currently transitioning forward towards a new chapter. Memories and emotions from the past rise up to the surface to be released. It does bring healing, and this creates space for the unique potential to flow into your life. You can prepare to forge a path that brings new wisdom and learning ahead. Your life has been an array of changes this year, and it has tested you on many levels. Strength is within you to overcome hurdles and expand your consciousness into new areas. You have been through some trials recently, and taking stock of your situation helps ground your energy. You discover you can take tentative steps to improve your circumstances. While expanding horizons may take you out of your comfort zone, the results are worthwhile. You find out you can maintain a sense of equilibrium while chasing your dreams. It marks a significant turning point that sees inspiration lighting a path forward. News ahead brings change. It does draw an inspirational aspect that captures your imagination, and it has you feeling excited about the potential. You touch down on developing an area that harnesses your emotions and creativity. This brings a time where you can move in alignment with your spirit. You share experiences with another and mark a significant turning point. It lets you take essential steps towards a brighter future. Being flexible opens the floodgates to a flow of grounding energy that restores balance.

The Full Moon in Aquarius at the beginning of this week is also a rare blue moon. A new understanding enters your world, which is restorative to your energy. There is some anxiety or unsettling energy that is holding you back. Knowing that you are being restricted helps you identify blocks and release limitations. This lets you open a dynamic new chapter. The power of change brings strength; it allows you to move forward away from uncertainty. Information arrives that brings clarity and confidence. A person in your social scene offers advice that is a big help. The past has been an extraordinary time of trials and tribulations. It has allowed you to gather wisdom and learn from experience. You are now in a position where you can share your knowledge with a broader audience. Change is arriving that takes you towards a nurturing environment and a productive time of new possibilities. It does seem a dream comes into focus, and this lights the path forward. In fact, it brings a catalyst for a change soon. You discover a therapeutic area, it heals wounds of the past and nurtures the creative magic within your spirit. There is an opportunity ahead to grow and develop your skills. It brings a path of learning and wisdom. Expanding your horizons draws dividends. You are entering a cycle of evolution that grows your abilities. It does let serendipity point the way forward. Fantastic options are set to be revealed that take you on a journey of building your talents and expanding your life. It brings exciting changes that offer a route forward. Happiness and abundance light the way towards achieving your vision. You make smart choices that let things come together nicely.

September 7th - New Moon in Virgo.

The Moon is on the same side of the Earth as the Sun and will not be visible in the night sky. This phase occurs at 00:52 UTC. This is an excellent time to observe galaxies and stars because there is no moonlight visible.

September 13 – First Quarter Moon in Sagittarius.

This Moon phase occurs at 20.39 UTC.

September 14th - Neptune at Opposition.

The giant blue planet will be at its closest approach to Earth, and its face will be illuminated by the Sun. This event occurs at 08:00 UTC.

September 14th - Mercury at Greatest Eastern Elongation.

The planet Mercury reaches greatest eastern elongation of 23.8 degrees from the Sun. This event occurs at 04:00 UTC. This is the best time to view Mercury. Look for the planet low in the western sky just after sunset.

September 20th - Full Moon in Pisces.

The Moon is on the opposite side of the Earth as the Sun and will be fully illuminated. This phase occurs at 23:55 UTC. Full Corn Moon. This Moon is also known as the Harvest Moon. The Harvest Moon is the full Moon that occurs closest to the September equinox each year.

September 22nd - September Equinox.

The 2021 September equinox occurs at 19:21 UTC. The Sun shines directly on the equator, creating equal amounts of day and night throughout the world. This is also autumnal equinox in the northern hemisphere and is considered a significant zodiac event for many traditional cultures.

September 27 – Mercury Retrograde begins in Libra.

During a retrograde period, it isn't the right time to move forward in any practical venture. Be prepared for misunderstandings and miscommunications to be more prevalent.

September 29 – Last Quarter Moon in Cancer.

This Moon phase occurs at 01.57 UTC.

The past is a time of stretching your resources and making do with what you had available. It has helped you advance your vision, it is now a time that fuels your ambition, and this leads to further progress. A new path opens and tempts you towards change. It does see you navigating a changing environment and coming up with roses. The crucial lessons learned can now be utilized to improve your circumstances. You unveil a new option that brings a boost to your goals and dreams. It is a fresh start that highlights the path of self-discovery. It does see confidence rising, purposeful energy is used to achieve gold. Exciting prospects surface, there is a buzz of activity ahead. The landscape is tinged with potential. You have weathered the storms and can enjoy smooth sailing into calmer waters.

You grow your life according to your values. It does see you continue to create your own opportunities and beat a path of your own innovative making. Life holds a refreshing twist, it signifies movement and discovery is swirling around the periphery of your life. It reveals new information that lets you discover a bold path forward. It does begin a voyage of that captures the essence of wanderlust. It does seem someone from the past is coming back into your life. It brings the time where choices are available. It does draw stabilizing energy that can enable the bond to improve with this person. Change is surrounding you on many levels. There may be something fresh on offer for your working life. A new role is pinpointed as opening a path; it has you feeling energized. A wise choice is made regarding your future. Focusing on strategy and planning draws exceptional results. It does see you are ready to step out and enjoy new options that grow your life.

Neptune at opposition occurs at the end of this week. Neptune rules your house of dreams and healing. The time is ripe for chasing your dreams and embracing a journey that enhances your creativity. Releasing the past does bring healing. Under this influence, you transform your potential, it is instrumental in bringing a new possibility to light. As you dismantle the blocks that keep you trapped in the past, you ignite change. It does see a new flow of energy is arriving. It helps you gain traction on expanding your social life. It connects you with a happy chapter that leaves you feeling a sense of renewal. You are headed towards an opportunity that could take your life in a new direction. It does let you set sail towards advancing your life. It heralds new beginnings and the essence of creation that lets you open the book on a new chapter. Your initiative makes waves, it does clear away the cobwebs and bring an avenue you can pursue with passion and enthusiasm. It brings adventures and excitement. The crossroads ahead does bring a turning point. It sweeps in changes that bring a positive aspect to your life. You uncover a direction that connects you to others you can mingle with. It draws the right kind of people into your life, and a curious new friendship soon blooms to life. A compelling path opens, and this brings an enchanting chapter. It connects you with a personal vision. A person makes specific thoughts and ideas known to you. It triggers a closer bond, and this leads to the expression and development of affection that is so valued. It does help you grow a personal relationship. The wheels are in motion, you gain a better understanding of where you stand with this person over the coming weeks. It does have you spending time with someone who shares your values.

You are given a boost when you notice synchronicity is guiding the path ahead. It creates a shift for your emotions that brings a positive and refreshing essence. This helps you quiet, restless vibrations, you get a greater sense that things are going to work in your favor. More balance and stability emerge, it does create the right environment for life to flow forward. Growth brings opportunities to mingle. There is someone new coming that helps grow your personal life, and this person brings exciting new experiences into your life. It does shine potential on developing a bond that leaves you feeling inspired. This is someone compatible, they are optimistic and happy. You embrace the fact that you click and get along beautifully with this individual. You are ready for a new chapter. In fact, fascinating opportunities are unearthed by your willingness to look beneath the surface and dig deeper into the potential possible in your world. Keeping an eye on the broader picture does draw a curious chapter that is the ticket towards nurturing your abilities. Change is part of the cycle of life, evolution is necessary, and it has the potential to reinvent your life. You can expect a few twists and turns as you navigate forward. Some are streamlining and rearranging necessary to bring goodness to the top. You are approaching a diverging path that opens a gateway towards an exciting possibility. It delivers news and excitement. It sets the stage for a new adventure. It brings a journey of self-development that reawakens your energy on many levels. It does allow you to push your boundaries back and enter a game-changing chapter of discovery.

The Equinox this week speaks of a golden opportunity arriving to inspire your mind and shift your focus forward. A bountiful chapter enters your life that brings abundance. It does chart an auspicious time that helps you really make your mark on the world. Against what has been an unsettling backdrop, you can expand your life and move forward towards exploring new options. There are no limits, your imagination is boundless. Explore all options and widen your focus. News arrives that taps into your endless creativity. It does bring a winning idea that lets you harness your free-spirited energy towards focusing on developing a dream project. A visionary aspect draws inspiration, you knuckle down and begin the process of bringing this potential to reality. As your vision takes concrete form, you reach a pinnacle that lets you see what your hard work has achieved. The path behind you has worn a track deep into your spirit. There have been many challenges that you have risen to meet and overcome. Your resilience and fortitude show that you are someone who never backs down. You push forward with purpose and achieve gold. This is all setting the stage to encourage you to continue to ascend and grow on this journey. As you ponder the next steps, information arrives to catch your interest. Travel is indicated in some form or another. It does bring new and exciting adventures. Sweeping changes come that expand your horizons, and it may see you seeking far-flung destinations. It does bring an exciting time where you grow and improve your life. It does see you go further as you harness your sense of fierce courage. It lets you plunge into deep waters that soothe your spirit. You form a solid alliance that draws dividends.

October 6 - New Moon in Libra.

The New Moon speaks of something new arriving in your world. This moon phase occurs at 11:05 UTC. This is an excellent time of the month to view galaxies and stars because there is no moonlight visible.

October 7 - Draconids Meteor Shower.

The Draconids meteor shower runs annually from October 6-10 and peaks this year on the night of the 7th.

October 8 – Mars in Conjunction with the Sun.

The planet Mars in Conjunction with the Sun. This occurs at 04:00 UTC.

October 9 – Mercury at Inferior Conjunction.

The planet Mercury at Inferior Conjunction. This planetary event occurs at 16:00 UTC.

October 13 – First Quarter Moon in Capricorn.

This Moon phase occurs at 03.25 UTC.

October 18 – Mercury Retrograde ends in Libra.

You can now move forward with any delayed plans that you have been putting off due to the Mercury Retrograde phase. Relationships should soon improve as miscommunications are overcome

October 20 - Full Moon in Aries.

The October full Moon is on the opposite side of the Earth as the Sun and will be fully illuminated. This phase occurs at 14:57 UTC. This full moon is known as the Hunters Moon. Powerful energy lights a path forward. You can attract and manifest excellent results during the complete moon phase.

October 21, 22 - Orionids Meteor Shower.

The Orionids meteor shower runs yearly from October 2 to November 7. Orionids meteor shower peaks this year on the night of October 21 and the morning of October 22.

October 25 - Mercury at Greatest Western Elongation.

The planet Mercury reaches greatest western elongation of 18.4 degrees from the Sun. Look for Mercury low in the eastern sky just before sunrise. This event occurs at 05:00 UTC.

October 28 – Last Quarter Moon in Leo.

This Moon phase occurs at 20.05 UTC.

October 29 - Venus Greatest Eastern Elongation.

The planet Venus reaches its greatest eastern elongation of 47 degrees from the Sun. This is the best time to view Venus. Look for the bright planet Venus in the western sky after sunset. This planetary phase occurs at 22.00 UTC.

Mercury retrograde delivers a message about finding balance within the hurricane. Life has thrown you a curveball, there may be some hold-ups that delay progress. Look for clues that surface at this time as it could lead to a significant turning point in your life. Discovering a path that opens the gateway forward does bring relief. It sees you heading ahead into the next cycle. There are a lot of dormant seeds that are ready to germinate, it does grow your potential. Something new and inspiring is happening for you soon. It does see exciting news arrive that heralds a fresh chapter. It brings a path of importance. It takes you towards expansion and opportunity. You soon get that feeling that things are falling into place. Luck and good fortune flow into your life when you need it the most. It does bring a new routine and changes that grow your potential. This is an especially potent time to improve your world because you are entering a cycle of optimism that lets the luck into your life. It does place you in an excellent position to soar to new heights. A venture you become involved with does take on a curious light. It brings a whole original path, one that feels like the right fit for your circumstances. Something is in the pipeline that lights up the trail of teamwork and technology. It does spark a fruitful collaboration, and it also brings colorful new characters into your life. It involves expanding your reach through networking, being involved with a social group. Exploring new methodologies that keep you in touch with others and being on the cutting edge of change does bring a new sense of confidence to your world.

Mars, in conjunction with the Sun this week, lets you pop the cork on the genie's bottle. You are ready to plant the prosperous seeds that unfold over the coming months. Opportunities are prepared to arrive. Setting intentions and staying positive does pave the way forward. You can feel proactive and take concrete action towards your vision. Soon an area you become involved with developing does become a reality. It stirs up exciting potential and delivers a beautiful adventure. When you look back at the past, it shines a light on just how far you have traveled on your personal journey. You have gained so much wisdom; there is much to appreciate in your current aspect. The lessons learned can be applied to improve your circumstances. It does let you adjust the bar higher, and this paves the way forward towards a rock-solid return on your energy. An area that you develop does connect you with a valued friend. There is good news on the aspect of developing interpersonal ties. It does see someone excitingly opening their thoughts. You move into a new territory and improve a personal situation. It does bring the forward motion that lets the bonding take shape. It does seem that this person currently hesitates on the precipice of change. It can feel like an unsettling time where you have your fair share of emotional surges. Your life can feel like a bit of a rollercoaster ride. Your life has had its share of ups and downs, you can now take advantage of the wisdom learned to apply these lessons to the coming chapter. It does see news arriving that draws a fresh start and lets you embrace the beginning of a brand-new episode.

Constraints are lifted when Mercury Retrograde ends this week; your situation expands outwardly.

This Full Moon in Aries brings emotional awareness. You may be feeling unsettled, and this relates to past events. It does signify a time of healing that helps you process and honor the feelings that arise. It brings a reflective phase that lets you resolve issues that may be holding you back. Gaining insight and wisdom into your deeper emotional awareness will help shape the path ahead. It brings rejuvenation and renewal. You may soon find yourself at the crossroads where a firm decision is required to take you in a new direction. Going within and contemplating the path ahead does provide you with the necessary guidance to choose wisely. You are transitioning to a new chapter that brings benefits. It shines a light on an expansive and optimistic journey forward. You are being gifted a green light to move forward towards developing your dreams. It does see a positive influence entering your world. It's the right time to let go of limitations that only cause disappointment. Adding fuel to your motivation sees inspirations skyrocket. It enables you to make a bold move towards achieving a long-held goal. The past has been a time of growing your abilities as you push back boundaries, set your sights on your goals, and nail them. The more you use your talents, the more life tempts you forward towards learning new areas. It gives you an expansive view of what is possible when you set your mind to it. A space you focus on is likely to come together and bring recognition and acclaim. Taking stock of the path ahead gives you a chance to catch your breath.

You find opportunities to join forces with others who support your journey forward. It gives you a leg up on creating an environment that brings stability into focus. You can broaden the scope of your imagination and harness creativity to stunning effect. A new chapter arrives soon. It provides you with a valuable gateway to growth. Being receptive to new possibilities lets you make the most of expanding your life towards a faster-moving environment. It is to your benefit as it leads to new interests and friendships. A moment of clarity provides insight into the path ahead that helps you channel your energy more effectively. It speaks about beautiful changes which are coming into your life soon. There are going to be attractive options that let you progress your goals. It has you enter into a dynamic time that attracts support from others who offer advice. It may even lead to collaboration. It brings a highly creative chapter that lets you dive in and explore a bevy of new options. You can shift your focus forward as an offer is coming soon that brings joy. It does provide you with advancement, you can utilize this situation to your advantage. Under a positive influence, you soon achieve an active phase of growth. You make a prominent name for yourself in a bustling new environment. This information is specifically pertinent and valuable to your vision. Growth and learning are highlighted as a useful accessory during this time. It brings a path that guides you forward by allowing you to trust in the process and let go of fixed expectations. It broadens your perception of what is possible, and it brings a lofty vision into focus.

November 4 - New Moon in Scorpio.

The New Moon brings a clean chapter of potential. This phase occurs at 21:15 UTC. This is an excellent time to view the stars because there is no moonlight visible.

November 5 - Uranus at Opposition.

The blue-green planet will be at its closest approach to Earth, and its face will be fully illuminated by the Sun. This event occurs at 00:00 UTC.

November 11 – First Quarter Moon in Aquarius.

This Moon phase occurs at 12.46 UTC.

November 12 - Taurids Meteor Shower.

The Taurids meteor shower runs yearly from September 7 to December 10. It peaks on the night of November 12.

November 17 - Partial Lunar Eclipse

A partial lunar eclipse occurs when the Moon passes through the Earth's partial shadow or penumbra, only a portion of it passes through the umbra. During this eclipse, part of the Moon darkens as it moves through the Earth's shadow. This partial lunar eclipse will be visible throughout most of eastern Russia, Japan, the Pacific Ocean, North America, Mexico, Central America, and parts of western South America.

November 17, 18 - Leonids Meteor Shower.

The Leonids meteor shower runs yearly from November 6-30. The Leonids meteor shower peaks this year on the night of the 17th and morning of the 18th.

November 19 - Full Moon in Taurus.

The Full Moon is on the opposite side of the Earth as the Sun and will appear fully illuminated. This phase occurs at 08:58 UTC. This full moon is known as Full Beaver Moon. Powerful energy lights a path forward. You can attract and manifest excellent results during the complete moon phase.

November 27 – Last Quarter Moon in Virgo.

This Moon phase occurs at 12.28 UTC.

November 29 – Mercury at Superior Conjunction.

The planet Mercury at Superior Conjunction. This planetary event occurs at 05:00 UTC.

The New Moon in Scorpio this week brings insight, clarity, and awareness. You see improvements arriving that bring a boost and set the stage for an exciting chapter where you can grow your goals. Clearing away limitations lets you move forward. Once you reveal what has hindered your progress, you reach a turning point. It allows you to chase a significant goal. You benefit from a lucky chapter. It does speak of personal projects and dreams coming into your life. It opens a path that holds a myriad of possibilities. It lets you blaze a trail forward, and this begins a transformational chapter. It is a time that leads to significant change, and this brings a boost to your confidence. It does leave you feeling hopeful about the future. It is a time where you can create space to focus on an area that inspires your mind. It brings the right opportunity to improve your circumstances. It draws an exciting and adventurous chapter that lifts the lid on exciting options. It brings a wellspring of possibility. If you have been feeling restless, this heightened activity is a fantastic area to explore. There are more opportunities to mingle and network. It does kick off a more social phase that brings new friendships to light. It's a time that draws a bustling aspect of the activity, and it does let the pace and rhythm of your life pickup. Being open to new experiences and people does see a window of opportunity opening. A sense of connection and harmony is ready to breeze into your life. Initiating social projects sets plans into motion that unfold into a path that inspires and delights. You can manifest your own happiness and progress in your abilities.

The Taurids meteor shower, which peaks on November 12th this year, see your potential shine brightly. Your star is rising; it's an exceptional time to plot a course towards a lofty endeavor. A new doorway appears and tempts you forward. You're ready to craft your vision and journey towards advancing a long-held goal. Being open to change helps you mark a significant turning point that sees potential skyrocket. It does bring a chapter that rules expansion and progression. You open the book on a new realm of possibilities. It does stir up exciting options to explore. This creates a gateway towards a new level of performance that draws recognition. It speaks of a shift forward that provides you with inspiration. It kicks off a chapter rejuvenation that brings new foundations. It lets you build dreams sustainably and securely. It sparks a productive chapter that has you using your creativity to stellar effect. You are currently transitioning towards a great new avenue. Using strategy and planning is essential as they help you take the proactive steps necessary to achieve your vision. You are blessed with a variety of gifts and talents. As you grow and evolve on your path, you peel back the layers of potential and reveal latent abilities ready to be used. Life offers you a chance to progress and develop your potential. It does let you explore a lesser worn path towards improving your experience. You blend your ideas and thoughts with others who understand you creatively. Taking it slow enables you to build foundations that are stable and secure. It's essential to move forward sustainably by being flexible, patient, and adaptable. This will draw the highest dividends. There is a lot of newness coming, keep dabbling in evolving the potential.

A Partial Lunar Eclipse on the 17th brings a landmark moment, it is a gateway toward a brighter future. This Lunar Eclipse speaks about a second chance. Helpful news arrives that the points the path forward. Some news is coming that brings great excitement. It lets you remove the limiting beliefs around security. Your vision gains momentum, you prioritize building a secure foundation and progressing towards the achievement of a long-held goal. You are focused and determined, your willingness to take a long term view draws dividends. You are in a time of transition. While it can feel unsettling, paying attention to the restlessness within your soul does open the pathway towards growth. It represents a time of reflecting on your dreams, desires, and goals. It does have you creating space to release all that prevents you from reaching a higher state of joy. Releasing limitations enables you to blaze through towards a journey that is self-expressive and joyful. Life is about to become happier and more expansive. Fundamental changes ahead draw positive energy; it lets you push back the barriers and embrace a more social environment. An invitation forward lets you mingle with friends. It does rebalance and rejuvenate your energy, and this draws improvement into your social life. It connects you with people you value. It does see a path opening that brings contentment and fulfillment. You can advance your vision through being mindful and utilizing a gift of manifestation. Set your intentions, plot the course you wish to achieve, and begin the process of taking the steps necessary to complete your vision. A quiet sense of satisfaction lets you feel proud.

Reflection and contemplation are valuable tools that help clear sensitive feelings. It is a favorable time to release blocks and focus on building grounded and stable energy. Staying flexible and adaptable allows you to weather any bumps in the road without becoming derailed. It does see a time of increasing stability that brings a grounded and secure base from which to develop your goals. There is a buzz of excitement that flows into your life soon as news arrives that inspires your mind. It does bring potential that unfurls gently over time. It brings you a shift forward that delivers new goals to contemplate. You soon enter uncharted territory and can plot a course towards a more social environment. It does transition you towards a journey that draws abundance. It brings a more expansive chapter that is exciting and adventurous. An invitation ahead allows you to mingle and network with other innovative trailblazers. You discover a penchant for creativity and feel ready to expand your horizons. This speaks about new options arriving. It does bring heightened social potential, you enjoy developing an alliance that is based on mutual respect. It does bring a chance to forge a bond with a companion who inspires your mind. As you unleash fresh possibilities in your social circle, it lets you dive into new adventures. The celebration ahead speaks of a lively and active environment. You can create stable foundations that bring emotional rewards. It does see you feeling comfortable and at home with progressing a bond of the heart. Things are finally flowing forward correctly for your own life. Insight into the path ahead illuminates a time of abundance, joy, and companionship.

December 4 - New Moon in Sagittarius.

The New Moon brings a clean slate of potential. This moon phase occurs at 07:43 UTC. This is an excellent time to view galaxies and stars because there is no moonlight visible.

December 4 – Total Solar Eclipse.

A total solar eclipse occurs when the moon completely blocks the Sun, revealing the Sun's outer atmosphere, which is called the corona. The path of totality will, for this eclipse, be limited to Antarctica and the southern Atlantic Ocean. A partial eclipse will bee visible throughout much of South Africa.

December 11 – First Quarter Moon in Pisces.

This Moon phase occurs at 01.36 UTC.

December 13, 14,15 - Geminids Meteor Shower.

The Geminids meteor shower runs each year from December 7-17. The Geminids meteor showers peaks this year on the night of the 13th, 14th, and 15th. The nearly new moon this year will provide dark skies for an excellent show. Best viewing will be from a dim vista after midnight. Meteors will radiate from the constellation Gemini but can appear anywhere in the sky.

December 19 - Full Moon in Gemini.

The Full Moon illuminates and draws clarity. This moon phase occurs at 04:36 UTC. This full moon is known as the Cold Moon and the Moon Before Yule. Powerful energy lights a path forward. You can attract and manifest excellent results during the full moon phase.

December 21 - December Solstice.

The 2021 December solstice occurs at 15:59 UTC. The South Pole of the earth tilts toward the Sun, which, having reached its most southern place in the sky, is directly over the Tropic of Capricorn at 23.44 degrees south latitude. This December solstice also marks the first day of winter in the Northern Hemisphere.

December 21, 22 - Ursids Meteor Shower.

The Ursids meteor shower occurs each year from December 17 - 25. This meteor event peaks this year on the night of the 21st and morning of the 22nd.

December 27 – Last Quarter Moon in Libra.

This Moon phase occurs at 02.24 UTC.

December hits the right kind of positive note that you need in your life. It is a favorable time to upgrade your dreams and chase your vision. Kindred spirits figure strongly into the weeks ahead. It does see you unwinding with your social circle, a celebration or significant social moment arrives to rejuvenate your life. This is a time that brings new options. It does encourage you to expand your consciousness and explore new possibilities. Under a more social sky, you discover there is room to spread your wings and embrace an active, connected environment. It does let you share thoughts and ideas with others, brainstorming sessions may even lead to a trailblazing path forward towards an innovative new area. Your efforts to improve your circumstances are likely to bear fruit. It does position you towards an exciting new chapter. As you continue to apply your abilities towards overcoming hurdles, you discover a new lead. It brings a bounty of new possibilities that shift your focus forward. This is an incredible harvest, it leads to a happy celebration where you spend time with friends and colleagues. The scene is set for a lively chapter ahead. New possibilities are revealed, it does bring a social and fast-paced environment that offers room to draw new friendships to light. It may also include distancing yourself from drama and from those who don't respect your boundaries. It is a process of streamlining your energy and bringing the cream to the top of your life. It brings a valuable sense of belonging, security, and stability. It does bring foundations that involve bonding and the merging of dreams. It does bring shifting priorities, change arrives that guides your progress forward.

News arrives that brings a boost to your morale. It does draw a situation closer and encourage the deepening of an interpersonal bond. It takes you towards the time of growth and developing goals that nurture emotions. It does place you in the right alignment to fan the fires of your inspiration. It connects you with someone who resonates on your wavelength. It speaks of a door opening that brings communication. It opens a path where you can push back barriers and embrace a more social environment. It does see an invitation ahead, drawing community involvement. It brings an upgrade to your home life that may feel subtle at first but does open pathways towards growth.

Indeed, things are set to improve in your life over the coming months. There is plenty of potential arriving over the forthcoming chapter. It does see long-term goals begin to take shape. You gain access to an area that offers room to progress and prosper. You are ready to create positive change. It has you moving away from a stormy backdrop that has been emotionally intense; you discover sunny skies are now overhead. It does bring positive energy and highlights difference is ahead. You benefit from a more socially active time in the weeks ahead. It does bring a chapter that is made for fun with friends and colleagues. An invitation to an engaging social experience is on the horizon. It does bring a lively crew of people together. Expanding your boundaries does see progress being made. A new friendship is forged in your broader social circle, and this sees much abundance is ready to blossom.

You have been dealing with integrating many changes in your life. It has been a destabilizing time where you may be questioning the path forward. There is a gateway that opens soon that lets you organize and streamline your goals. It helps you decode the road ahead and brings a new chapter to your door. It does offer a solid foundation that draws security into your life. There is a focus on healing the past and creating space to prosper in a new environment. You can release the heaviness, and shadows and transition towards a brighter chapter. You can ascertain a path forward if you have been dealing with more burdens then you would like, release your hurdles to the universe. You are ready to face a lighter future that does draw a new friendship into your world. Essential changes are set to occur. You unearth an option that encourages you to explore a path forward. It depicts a time that brings happiness. There are smiles all round when fortune shines upon your life. A venture you contribute to does bring new friends and colleagues into your circle. It does establish your talents in an area that helps advance your vision further. It has you dreaming big about future possibilities. You are entering the highly social aspect, and this draws signs and serendipity into your life. As you network and mingle, you bring a new friendship to light that does spark your interest. It leads to a flight of fancy as it brings new options into your love life. It triggers a path of expanding your opportunities and becoming open to change. It does seem there is responsive and open communication based on developing this bond. This reflects the sunshine which seeks to come into your world.

You are set to enter an optimistic chapter, it offers you options to circulate, this social growth does inspire a light-hearted environment. It has you spending time with friends and family. It stirs terrific conversations with others, it draws blessings and abundance into your life. Exciting opportunities are ready to roll into your world, it does bring a theme that touches down on connecting with kindred spirits. You become involved in an area that offers a chance to network and grows your social circle. Forging new contacts does bring friendships to light; it sees you working beautifully with people of a similar mindset. It does bring a communal effort; a shared vision is at the basis of this chapter. Your sense of purpose holds you in good stead, it directs your energy towards achieving the results you seek. It speaks about some unusual changes occurring that open a path that draws excitement. It ushers in a time of change and sparks inspiration, it becomes a big focus for you moving forward. You are headed towards the time of opportunity that could take your life in a new direction. It does outline a journey towards abundance as you light up areas that speak to your heart. Following your inspiration is the short ticket to success. Your dreams are within reach; taking a courageous step towards planning lofty goals draws inspiration and adventure into your life. Things are turning full-circle. This outlines a path that leaves you feeling excited and inspired about the possibilities. As your situation flows forward, it brings a portal, a new chapter, this transitions you to an environment that is ripe with potential. There are indications that hidden information comes to light that brings a happy realization.

Dear Stargazer,

I hope you have enjoyed planning your year with the stars utilizing Astrology and Zodiac influences. You can also get personal astrology or intuitive readings by contacting me via social media.

https://www.facebook.com/SiaSands

Instagram: SiaSands

Get a reading here:

https://psychic-emails.com/

Leaving a review is welcomed and appreciated.

Many Blessings,

Sia Sands